Look out for these other exciting titles from Book House

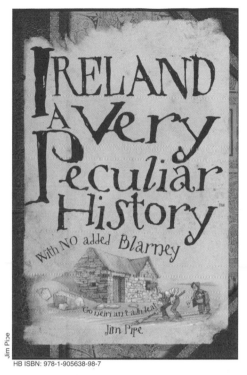

Jim Pipe

HB ISBN: 978-1-905638-98-7

# CHERISHED LIBRARY

The Cherished Library is a new series, designed to look and feel like classics from a distinguished library.

*Ireland: A Very Peculiar History* is a lively and informative account of the history of the whole island of Ireland, from its earliest inhabitants to the present day. It celebrates the cultural achievements of the Irish, and recounts as objectively as possible the turbulent political events that have helped to shape today's Ireland and Northern Ireland.

*Scotland: A Very Peculiar History* is a lively and informative account, in two volumes, of the vibrant history of Scotland, from its earliest inhabitants to the present day. It celebrates Scottish achievements, giving an up-to-date and objective account of the nation's history, with 'No added Haggis'.

- Black-and-white line illustrations with full-colour endpapers
- Hardback    £6.99 each vol.
- 152 x 101 mm; 192pp

- Interest 8-80+; Reading age 8+
- KS 2/3
- Gold foiling
- Gloss lamination
- Embossing

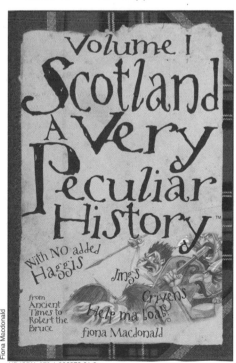

Fiona Macdonald

HB ISBN: 978-1-906370-91-6

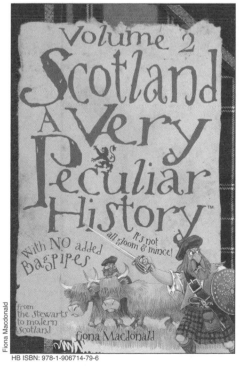

Fiona Macdonald

HB ISBN: 978-1-906714-79-6

Scotland Vol. 1

Ireland

Available from all good bookshops
www.book-house.co.uk
or, for a catalogue, write to Book House, 25 Marlborough Place, Brighton, BN1 1UB

# CONTENTS

Author and artist:
**Mark Bergin** studied at Eastbourne College of Art and has specialised in historical reconstructions, aviation and maritime subjects for over 20 years. He lives in Bexhill-on-Sea with his wife and three children.

Additional artists: **John James** and **Gerald Wood**

Series creator and designer: **David Salariya**

Editor: **Karen Barker Smith**

Assistant Editor: **Michael Ford**

With thanks to The Ermine Street Guard, Gloucester, England.

Published in Great Britain in MIII by
Book House, an imprint of
**The Salariya Book Company Ltd**
25 Marlborough Place, Brighton BN1 1UB

SALARIYA

Visit our website at **www.book-house.co.uk**
or go to **www.salariya.com**
for **free** electronic versions of:
**You Wouldn't Want to be an Egyptian Mummy!**
**You Wouldn't Want to be a Roman Gladiator!**
**Avoid Joining Shackleton's Polar Expedition!**
**Avoid Sailing on a 19th-Century Whaling Ship!**

ISBN 978-1-906714-96-3

A catalogue record for this book is available from the British Library.

Printed and bound in China.
Printed on paper from sustainable forests.

Reprinted with new cover MMIX

Photographic credits
t=top b=bottom c=centre l=left r=right

Ancient Art and Architecture Collection: 21tr, 37bl
The Art Archive/ British Museum/ Dagli Orti: 10
The Art Archive/ Musée du Louvre/ Dagli Orti: 14, 15
The Art Archive/ Staatliche Glypohtek Munich/ Dagli Orti (A): 35
Mark Bergin: 42
Bildarchiv Steffens/ Bridgeman Art Library: 33
Bresslich and Foss: 40
David Stewart: 32, 34, 35, 36
Digital Stock/ Corbis corporation: 6b, 7tl, 26
Doug Smith: 28tr, 36tl, 37c
E. Hobson/ Ancient Art and Architecture Collection: 17
Egytpian National Museum, Cairo/ Bridgeman Art Library: 17b
John Foxx Images: 12, 18, 19
Louvre, Paris, France/ Bridgeman Art Library: 7tr
Mountain High Map/ copyright 1993 Digital Wisdom Inc: 6/7
Staatliche Museen zu Berlin – Preussicher Kulturbesitz, Antikerammlung/ bpk photo: Johanes Laurnetiiub, 2002: 21l
Wadsworth Atheneum, Hartford/ J. Pierpont Morgan Collection/ Joseph Szaszfai: 20

Every effort has been made to trace copyright holders. The Salariya Book Co. apologises for any unintentional omissions and would be pleased, in such cases, to add an acknowledgement in future editions.

PAPER FROM SUSTAINABLE FORESTS

# BATTLE ZONES

# WARFARE
## IN THE
# ANCIENT WORLD

Written and illustrated
by Mark Bergin

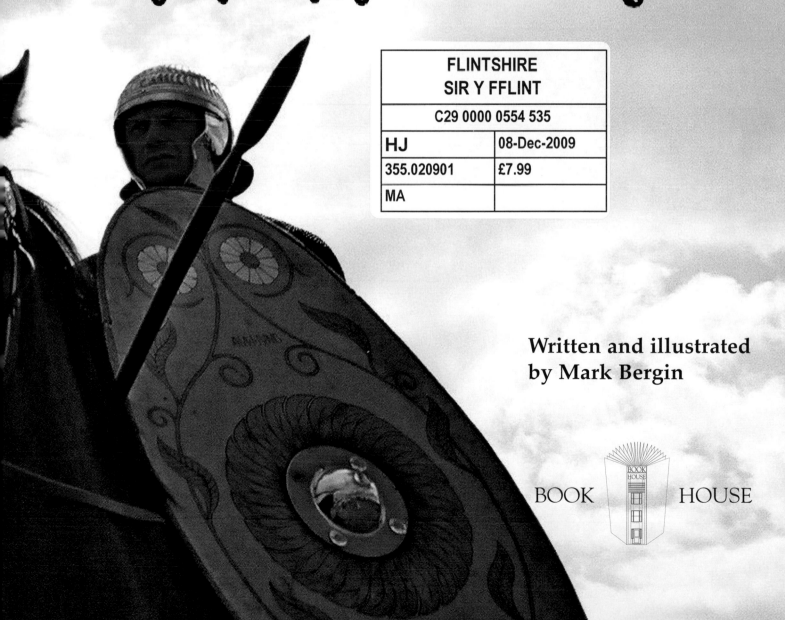

BOOK HOUSE

# THE ANCIENT WORLD

The first civilisations arose in the fertile lands around the major rivers of the Near East. As these societies grew they shared many common features: the development of government, writing, cities and grand public buildings. Food production increased with irrigation so fewer people were needed for farming. This resulted in more people moving to towns and cities as craftsmen and traders. As the cities grew they became power bases for rulers. Central governments were created, controlling armies, trade and food production. Legal systems were developed and distinct classes began to form within society. As populations grew larger they came into conflict over land, trade routes and resources.

## THE ROMANS

The Romans established a republic in 510 BC which gradually expanded its power with the use of military force. They conquered the highly civilised Greeks to the east and brought civilisation to the Celtic tribes of the north and west. The Romans dominated the western world for over 500 years (31 BC to AD 565). Under *Pax Romana* – the Roman peace – law, order and prosperity were brought to bear across the Empire.

*Temple at Abu Simbel, Egypt (right)*

*Parthenon, in Athens, Greece*

## THE GREEKS

Greek power stemmed from the formation of city-states or *poleis*. These independent, self-governing communities fought for land and trade routes and against invasions by the expanding Persian Empire to the east. After the Peloponnesian War (431-404 BC) the Greek city-states were brought together by Alexander the Great.

## THE PERSIANS

In 550 BC Cyrus, the prince of Persia, united the peoples of Medes and Persia to make Iran the dominant power in Asia and the Near East. Successful military campaigns increased his empire until it incorporated the Middle East, the Ionian Greek settlements of Asia Minor, Babylon and Afghanistan. After around 100 years of stability, Persia was attacked and eventually defeated by the Greeks, led by Alexander the Great, in 331 BC.

## THE EGYPTIANS

The power of the ancient Egyptian civilisation lasted for over 3,000 years. Successive pharaohs expanded out from the Nile valley into the Middle East and Asia with large, well-trained armies. By the Middle Kingdom (2040-1790 BC) large fortresses had been built to guard the frontiers of Egypt in the south and east.

## THE ASSYRIANS

From around the 10th century BC to the 7th century BC the Assyrian Empire was the dominant military power in the Near East. At the height of its power, under King Ashurbanipal (668-627 BC), the Empire stretched from Egypt in the west to the borders of Iran in the east.

*Sumerian chariot of King Eannatum of Lagash, c. 2500 BC*

SUMERIAN CHARIOT
This lumbering four-wheeled chariot (below) was drawn by onagers (wild asses). Such chariots were probably used as troop carriers rather than fighting platforms.

# ARMIES OF THE EAST

Power ebbed and flowed between various kingdoms as they fought over the region's fertile lands, trade routes and gold and silver deposits. Some societies grew under strong leadership, others prospered through military skill. When several warring states were at last united by the King of Ur in 2500 BC, they became known as the Sumerians. The Sumerians were the first civilisation to use chariots and infantry in battle formation.

The Hittites, a people from the mountains of Armenia, had conquered Syria and Palestine by 1343 BC. They used iron weapons which gave them a great advantage over enemies still using bronze because iron is stronger than bronze. The Sumerians called iron 'metal from Heaven' because of the advantages iron weapons had in battle.

The Syrians were at the height of their power in the 10th and 9th centuries BC, until they split into warring kingdoms. The best known of these was Damascus.

This archer (below) has a triangular composite bow and distinctive, geometric patterned, clothing. This image is based on one seen on a vizier's tomb in Thebes, Egypt.

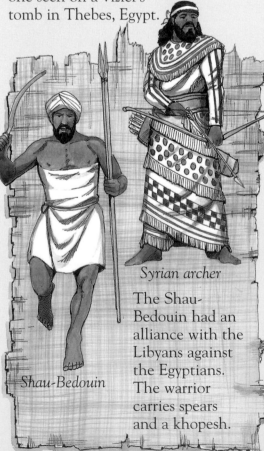

*Shau-Bedouin*

*Syrian archer*

The Shau-Bedouin had an alliance with the Libyans against the Egyptians. The warrior carries spears and a khopesh.

Sea Peoples
warrior

Libyan
archer

Semite
archer

Hittite
guard

The Semites, also known as Israelites, occupied the region around Jordan and the Dead Sea. This archer (above) holds typical weapons – a bow and a duck-billed axe.

The Sea Peoples invaded Egypt in 1190 BC. They were driven back by Rameses III and eventually settled in towns around Palestine.

This Hittite (above) wears the kilt of a royal guard. His crested helmet indicates his rank. Other Hittite soldiers wore long, short-sleeved tunics.

Libyan tribes were known for their military skill. They had many conflicts with the Egyptians but also served as mercenaries in the pharaohs' armies.

## HITTITE CHARIOT

War chariots were commonly used in battles between the Hittites and Egyptians. Each chariot had a three-man crew: a driver, a shield bearer and an armoured spear-man. Rameses II called the Hittites *humty* (women soldiers) due to the way they wore their hair.

Hittite
chariot

# THE ASSYRIAN ARMY

The organisation, efficiency and effectiveness of the Assyrian army had no equal until the rise of the legions of Rome. After suffering four centuries of domination by the Babylonian and Hittite empires, the Assyrian attitude to outsiders hardened. On battle campaigns they attacked their enemies intent on extermination or forced resettlement. At its height, under King Ashurbanipal (ruled 668-627 BC), the Assyrian army must have struck terror into its opponents. The well-trained and well-armed force could field 20,000 foot soldiers, 12,000 cavalry and 1,200 two-horse chariots. Their daggers and swords were made of iron – creating stronger weapons than those their opponents had. In sieges the Assyrian force used six-wheeled assault towers each equipped with an iron-tipped battering ram. After King Ashurbanipal's death, the Empire collapsed under the rule of weaker kings and was once more taken over by the Babylonians.

ARMED FORCES
Assyrian archers, infantry and cavalry (opposite) all wore the same standard bronze-plate body armour and iron helmets. Warhorses were protected by tough fabric armour.

CAPTIVES
The Assyrians were ruthless in war. Their treatment of captives was notorious – they were impaled on stakes or flayed alive. When Assyrian King Shalmanaser planned to sell 10,000 enemy soldiers as slaves he first had them blinded.

*This relief (left) discovered in Nimrud (in present day Iraq) shows an Assyrian attack on an enemy village.*

Assyrian war chariots (right) were so
heavy that each needed four horses
to pull it. Such chariots proved to
be decisive weapons in the battle at
Halule in 691 BC. After the demise
of the Assyrian Empire, the chariot
design was adopted by the Babylonian
forces of Nebuchadnezzar II.

*Heavy chariot of Ashurbanipal,*
*7th century BC*

*Archer*

*Infantryman*
*c. 655 BC*

*Cavalryman*
*c. 655 BC*

11

# AGE OF THE PHARAOHS

*T*hrough the arid landscape of Egypt runs the River Nile. Every year the river overflows its banks, flooding the land on either side. This 'inundation' brings life-giving water and rich riverbed nutrients to the soil and it allowed the ancient Egyptians to grow food for themselves with enough left to export. The region was also rich in gold, copper and quality building stone and Egypt became wealthy.

For over 3,000 years, the kings of Egypt were given the title pharaoh, which means 'great house'. The ancient Egyptians believed that the pharaohs were living gods and this was reflected in the construction of their fantastic tombs, the great pyramids. The pharaohs had supreme power, with governors and officials on hand to carry out their will. Pharaohs developed an efficient and well-organised army to expand Egypt's borders and protect against enemies.

*Ancient Egypt*

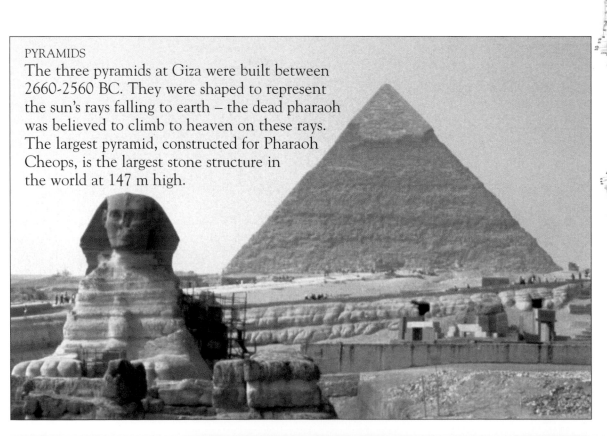

PYRAMIDS
The three pyramids at Giza were built between 2660-2560 BC. They were shaped to represent the sun's rays falling to earth – the dead pharaoh was believed to climb to heaven on these rays. The largest pyramid, constructed for Pharaoh Cheops, is the largest stone structure in the world at 147 m high.

Border
fort

Bedouin tribes

Giza

Memphis

River Nile

Western Desert

Red Sea

Eastern
Desert

Thebes

Karnak

Nubian
warriors

Valley of the Kings

Philae

# THE EGYPTIAN ARMY

In the New Kingdom period (1567-1085 BC) the ancient Egyptian army was well structured, with a strong chain of command. As a new recruit, a peasant volunteer or conscript was taken down the River Nile to a vast training camp near the city of Memphis. Here he was taught to march and learned skills such as fighting with a sword and shield, archery, battle tactics and chariot driving. Once their training was complete, recruits joined an army division.

## PYRAMID OF COMMAND

The pharaoh was the overall commander of the Egyptian army. His generals were division commanders and beneath them were officers in control of smaller units. The army also needed skilled doctors, scribes and priests.

An officer's rank was shown by his baton (below). The baton was also useful for disciplining recruits.

*Officer*

## WEAPONS

The khopesh (right) was a curved sword adopted by the Egyptians from the Hyksos. The Hyksos invaded and conquered parts of Egypt during the second intermediate period (1790-1550 BC). They also introduced scale armour, composite bows and horse-drawn battle chariots to the Egyptians.

*Khopesh*

## ARMY DIVISIONS

Every army division had around 5,000 men, 4,000 of whom were foot soldiers. The remaining 1,000 were charioteers who fought with bows and spears.

## DAILY PRACTICE

Wrestling (above) kept the soldiers fit and agile. Drilling and marching kept up discipline and stamina. Soldiers learned to act on trumpet signals to charge and retreat.

## GUARDING THE EMPIRE

The fortification at Semnah (below) was built in the New Kingdom period as part of a line of forts designed to repel invasions from the Sea Peoples and the Libyans.

## NUBIAN ARCHERS

Nubians (right) were mercenaries, professional soldiers employed by the pharaoh. They were valued for their skills as archers. Their chiefs wore ostrich feathers, large gold earrings and collars as signs of their rank.

*Nubian archers*

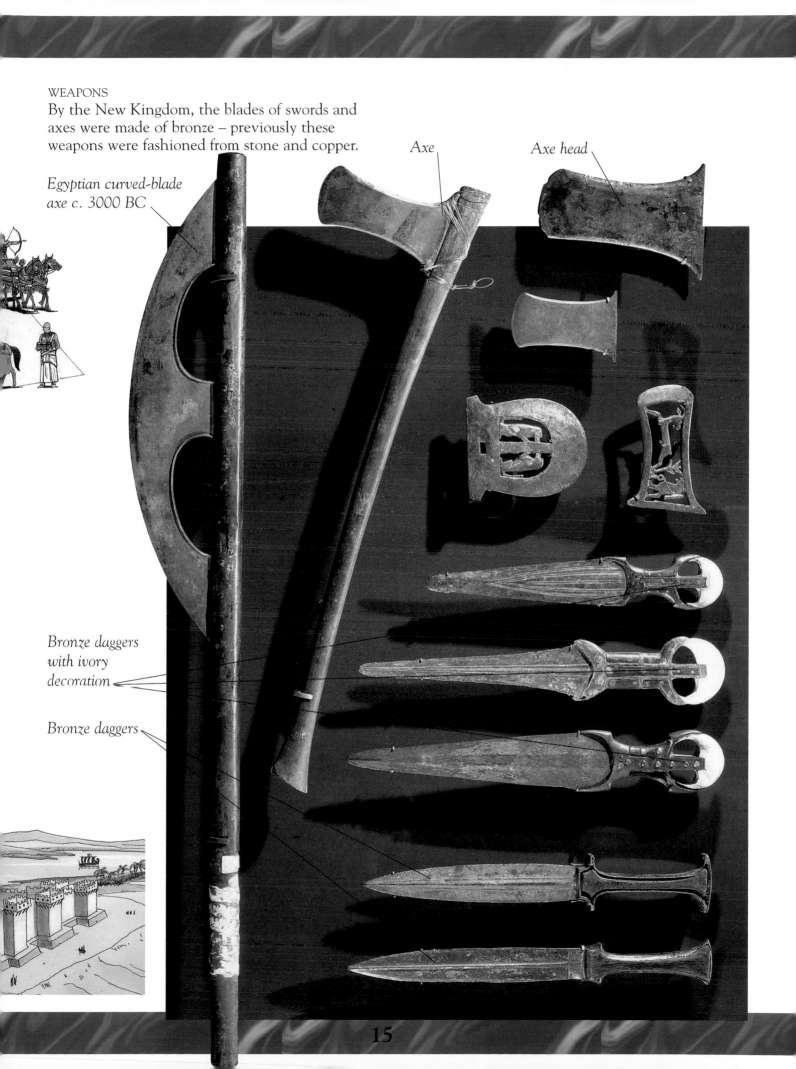

WEAPONS
By the New Kingdom, the blades of swords and axes were made of bronze – previously these weapons were fashioned from stone and copper.

Axe

Axe head

*Egyptian curved-blade axe c. 3000 BC*

*Bronze daggers with ivory decoration*

*Bronze daggers*

# SHOCK TACTICS

The fast, light and manoeuvrable chariot became a devastating weapon in ancient Egypt. Introduced by the Hyksos, the Egyptians developed their own tactics for the best use of the chariots in battle. They were used as mobile fighting platforms for archers, assaulting the enemy's front line from a distance and breaking up the infantry before Egyptian troops attacked.

*Slinger*

Slingers (left) were used to soften up the enemy from long range.

*Infantryman*

Infantrymen wore leather chest protection and carried a shield and khopesh.

Archers were used en masse. They wore no body protection as they were not expected to be close to the enemy.

*Archer*

Often the first conflict between chariot forces dictated the victor of an entire battle. In 1288 BC, at the Battle of Kadesh, Egyptian chariots lead by the Pharaoh Rameses II won the engagement with the Hittite chariots resulting in the Hittite infantry not entering the battle at all.

## CHARIOTS

Chariots in the New Kingdom period (below) were lightweight to allow maximum speed and manoeuvrability. The rear axle was extra long to give greater stability for sharp turns.

*Archers depicted on the walls of the temple of Rameses III at Medinet Habu, Egypt (above)*

*Egyptian battle chariot from the New Kingdom period*

## HORSES

Chariot horses (left) were protected by brightly covered fabric or leather armour. Quivers full of arrows were mounted on either side of the chariot for ease of use. The forward facing case contained two bows and a hand axe.

## HUNTING

The carving on this ostrich-feather fan handle (below) shows the King Tutankhamun hunting ostriches in a chariot. Hunting was good practice for charioteers and archers.

*Wood and gold ostrich-feather fan handle from Tutankhamun's tomb, c.1340 BC*

# CITY-STATES

*Athena*

About 2,500 years ago the peoples of Greece formed the first great civilisation in mainland Europe. Most ancient Greeks lived in communities known as 'city-states'. Each city-state consisted of a small, self-governing city and the surrounding countryside that it controlled. There were many city-states in ancient Greece and they were all fiercely independent. Each had its own fighting force and conflicts were common due to their expanding populations and a shortage of good farmland. This resulted in some city-states becoming more powerful, particularly Athens and Sparta. In addition to internal conflict the ancient Greeks suffered two invasions by the Persians. On both occasions, the Greeks fought hard campaigns, defeated the Persians and forced them to withdraw.

Between 447-438 BC the Athenians built the Parthenon (below). The temple was built as thanks to their goddess Athena (left) for their victory over the Persians.

*The Parthenon*

## THE ASSEMBLY IN ATHENS

The golden age of Greek city-states such as Athens was between 479-431 BC. Great progress was made in the sciences, the arts, sport and politics. *Demokratia* is a Greek word meaning 'rule of the people' and it was in the city-state of Athens that democracy was born. The Assembly in Athens met every nine days, when Athenian citizens could have their say and vote on important matters. Around 5,000 citizens regularly attended, so Assembly meetings were often noisy and argumentative.

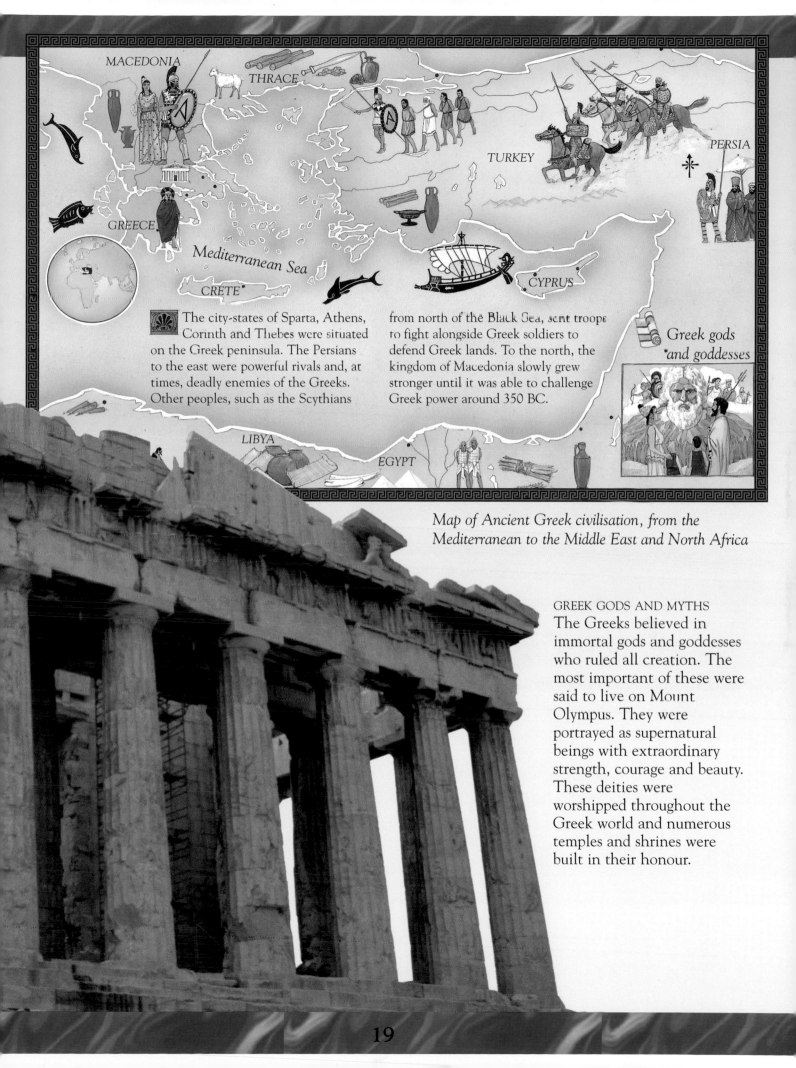

MACEDONIA

THRACE

TURKEY

PERSIA

GREECE

Mediterranean Sea

CRETE

CYPRUS

The city-states of Sparta, Athens, Corinth and Thebes were situated on the Greek peninsula. The Persians to the east were powerful rivals and, at times, deadly enemies of the Greeks. Other peoples, such as the Scythians from north of the Black Sea, sent troops to fight alongside Greek soldiers to defend Greek lands. To the north, the kingdom of Macedonia slowly grew stronger until it was able to challenge Greek power around 350 BC.

*Greek gods and goddesses*

LIBYA

EGYPT

*Map of Ancient Greek civilisation, from the Mediterranean to the Middle East and North Africa*

GREEK GODS AND MYTHS
The Greeks believed in immortal gods and goddesses who ruled all creation. The most important of these were said to live on Mount Olympus. They were portrayed as supernatural beings with extraordinary strength, courage and beauty. These deities were worshipped throughout the Greek world and numerous temples and shrines were built in their honour.

The best cavalry were men from the northern state of Thessaly where fine horses were bred and there was a tradition of good horsemanship.

Cavalrymen normally came from wealthy families because of the high cost of owning horses.

*Scythian archer*

*Cavalryman*

*Greek hoplite*

From the 7th century BC, hoplites fought in a phalanx formation. They lined up together, up to eight men deep, and advanced with spears pointing towards the enemy. Officers and generals were expected to fight in the front row of the phalanx.

Spartans were the most feared warriors in ancient Greece. Boys were taken from their families at the age of seven to be sent to barracks, where they learnt discipline and the value of exercise. This 6th-century bronze figure (above) is believed to be of a Spartan officer.

# GREEK WARRIORS

Hoplites fought with long spears and swords. They held large round shields called argives and were protected by crested bronze helmets, breast plates and greaves.

This bronze figure (below) portrays a typical hoplite but is missing his spear. Notice his long hair flowing from under the helmet.

*Arm positioned to hold a spear*

*Crest*

*Bronze helmet*

*Argive*

*Greave*

This Greek relief carving (above) shows hand-to-hand fighting. The warriors hold large bronze shields with grips around the rim.

Greek city-states were rivals for trade and land and were often at war. Sparta was dedicated to warfare – all its male citizens were soldiers and the city was run like an army camp. The Athenians expected all male citizens over the age of 17 to defend their homeland and when the government called them to fight it was regarded as a great honour. The majority of the Athenian army were foot soldiers called hoplites. These were mainly recruited from farming families wealthy enough to afford the necessary armour and weapons. On becoming a soldier they swore an oath, to defend 'the wheat, the barley, the vines, the olives and figs.' Wars in this period were often short because men had to be home in time for the harvest – if crops were not harvested then the entire state suffered a lack of food.

# WAR AT SEA

The Athenian navy played a vital part in Athen's empire-building around the Aegean Sea. The navy recruited over 20,000 free men, mostly those who could not afford the armour necessary to be a hoplite.

The three main types of Greek warships were known as penteconters, biremes and triremes.

A penteconter was a galley with 50 oarsmen; biremes had two rows of oars, one above the other; and triremes had a total of 170 oarsmen. Triremes also had one large mast with a sail. Before a battle, the sail and rigging were taken down and the trireme was powered by the oarsmen.

*Hoplite*

FIGHTING AT SEA
A trireme's fighting force were heavily armoured hoplites (left). They boarded enemy ships or defended their own from the upper deck.

This vase decoration (far left) shows a bireme setting sail. At the stern are two steering oars and a ladder, used as a gangplank by the crew.

## BATTLE OF SALAMIS

One of the most important Greek victories at sea was against the Persians at the Battle of Salamis in 480 BC. The Greeks had only 300 triremes against 800 Persian ships. The Greek fleet retreated into narrow channels around the island of Salamis. The Persians followed but their fleet was so large that there was no room for manoeuvre. The Greeks attacked the Persians, ramming their ships and forcing a retreat.

## BATTLE TACTICS

A favoured trireme tactic was to sail straight at the enemy amidships, ramming a hole and sinking the vessel. Triremes also sailed close alongside, smashing the enemy's oars with the bronze prow. This left the enemy ship helpless and vulnerable to boarding or ramming. A brazier was kept onboard Greek ships to provide burning torches and arrows. When fired at an enemy ship, the vessel was set alight, causing its crew to panic.

*Trireme ramming another vessel with its bronze prow*

Triremes were rowed by 170 oarsmen – 85 men on each side. Skilful teams could propel a trireme for short periods at 16 km/h.

*Oarsmen*

The heavy bronze prow of a trireme also projected underwater. Often a huge eye was painted on the side of the ship (left) to ward off evil.

*Prow*

# AGE OF CONQUEST

Alexander III became King of Macedonia, the most powerful state in Greece, in 336 BC. Many Greek states were weakened after the long Peloponnesian War (431-404 BC). Alexander's father, Philip II, had seized the opportunity to make himself master of all Greece, but was murdered at the height of his power. Alexander made the most of the power base left by his father and became the supreme military commander of his day, known as Alexander the Great. His speed and decisiveness made him a great general. He insisted on leading his men in battle, sharing the dangers and discomforts of campaigns and this inspired loyalty from his men during the long years of his conquests. In 13 years, with only around 35,000 troops, Alexander defeated the vast Persian Empire and conquered lands in Asia Minor, Egypt and India.

Map of Alexander the Great's conquests 334-225 BC

Alexander finally destroyed the Persian army at the Battle of Gaugamela in 331 BC. He went on to sweep through Egypt into India.

Alexander's favourite horse, a present from his father, was called Bucephalus, meaning 'ox-head'. Shortly after Alexander defeated an Indian army at the Battle of Hydaspes in 326 BC, Bucephalus died. Alexander decided to found a city, Bucephala, on the spot where his faithful horse was buried. After Hydaspes, Alexander's exhausted troops refused to go any further, forcing him to return to Persia.

Alexander was taken ill, with what was probably malaria, and he died, aged 32, in Babylon on his way home.

*Roman bust of Alexander the Great (356–323 BC), copied from a Greek statue of 338 BC*

# THE ROMANS

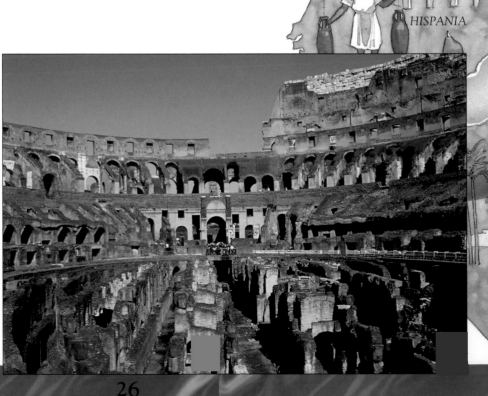

*Map showing the Roman Empire*

Londiniu

HISPANIA

Around 510 BC, Rome began to develop from a small town into a busy city. Roman citizens fought successfully to control vital trade routes throughout southern Italy and gained land. Rome's rise to power would have been impossible without an efficient, well-organised and loyal army. Around 270 BC, the army began to conquer neighbouring regions and by 50 BC Rome's generals had marched northwards and conquered much of Germania (present day Germany) and Gaul (France). The Romans invaded Britain in AD 43. From AD 106-116 Rome overran the Middle East and by AD 117 the Roman Empire encircled the whole of the Mediterranean Sea, covering large areas of Europe, the Near East and Africa. All conquered lands sent goods and money to Rome as tribute and taxes. In return, the Empire provided a stable, relatively peaceful society, good laws and profitable trade. Its professional army provided soldiers to man forts all around the frontiers, defending from attacking tribes and bordering kingdoms. Roman imperial power lasted almost five centuries until Rome was sacked in AD 410 by Alaric the Visigoth. The Empire finally collapsed around AD 476 when the last western emperor was deposed.

Symbols of ancient Rome's power can still be seen today. All over the Empire the Romans created great structures, from the Colosseum (right) and Forum in Rome to the Pont du Gard in France and Hadrian's Wall in Britain. These provide an insight into the lives of the Romans, their government and their conquests.

GERMANIA

GAUL

Roman Empire's
frontier

DACIA

Black Sea

ITALY

Rome

Naples

GREECE

Mediterranean Sea

SICILY

Carthage

CRETE

CYPRUS

AFRICA

EGYPT

# ENEMIES OF ROME

*Roman coin showing a barbarian on horseback*

The Roman Empire met resistance from a variety of cultures and armed forces. By Roman standards the Germanic peoples of northern Germany were uncivilised and the Romans called them 'barbarians'. They lived in tribes and were always fighting among themselves for territory. This made it easier for the well-disciplined Roman soldiers to defeat them. In the 5th century BC, present day France, Belgium and Britain were inhabited by Celtic tribes, called *Galli* or Gauls. They were skilled metalworkers, but their iron weapons could not stop the Romans. By 51 BC, Julius Caesar had conquered the whole area.

*Germanic and Dacian (Romanian) warriors from the 1st -2nd century AD*

### A BARBARIAN VICTORY

Rome was not always victorious. In a battle at Teutoburger forest (western Germany) in AD 9 the barbarians destroyed three Roman legions. Following this defeat the Romans relied on a line of forts along the rivers Rhine and Danube to keep the barbarians at bay.

### IBERIAN AND HISPANIC WARRIORS

The ancient peoples of the area now known as Spain were formidable warriors (left). They fought against Rome in the three Punic wars between 265-146 BC. The Romans invaded because the land was fertile and rich in gold and silver deposits.

*Iberian and Hispanic warriors, 2nd century BC*

British chariots were extremely fast and manoeuvrable. Warriors could fight from the chariot or dismount to fight on foot. Fully-armed noblemen carried a shield, spear and helmet.

Gallic warriors wore chain mail shirts over their tunics or sometimes fought naked! Some bronze helmets were decorated with boars or eagles, thought to give the wearer extra courage.

*Celtic chariot*

*Horsehair crest*

*Gallic warriors*

*Parthian horse archer*

The Parthians (left) were a nomadic people who conquered a large area of territory from Armenia to Afghanistan. One tactic the Parthians used was to gallop at the enemy's infantry in formation. About 90 m from the enemy, the riders wheeled around, shooting two or three arrows at the same time. This became known as a 'Parthian shot'.

The Persians' (below) original homeland was northeast of the Persian Gulf. They conquered the Parthians in the 3rd century BC and went on to challenge the Roman Empire's frontier east of the Euphrates river.

*Persian cavalryman*

# THE ROMAN ARMY

There were around 30 legions in the Roman army, made up of infantrymen and auxiliaries such as archers and cavalry. Each legion had its own name, number, badge and command base or fort. Legions were posted throughout the Empire and were self-sufficient, each with their own commanders and ranking officers, ordinary soldiers and specialists, including doctors and engineers. In peacetime, soldiers trained and were put to work building forts and roads. The legions also acted as local government in the regions where they were posted.

## A LEGION
Every legion was divided into units and ranks. This meant that troops could be easily organised and controlled and orders could be carried out quickly and efficiently.

Optio

Standard bearer

Centurion

Cavalry officer

A cohort was made up of six centuries. There were ten cohorts in a legion.

A century was 80 men (ten conturbeniums) commanded by a centurion.

Conturbeniums were the smallest units of the army, each consisting of eight men who cooked, ate and shared a tent together.

CHAIN OF COMMAND
The *legatus*, or legate, was the commander of the legion. Below him were six officers, called tribunes, from Rome's most aristocratic families. Then came the *praefectus castrorum* or second-in-command. Under him was the *primus pilus* or chief centurion. Normal centurions each had a deputy called an *optio* and at the bottom of the chain was the legionary. New recruits joined the army as legionaries and could work their way up to the rank of praefectus castrorum.

CHAIN OF COMMAND

*Legatus*

*Tribunes*

*Praefectus castrorum*

*Primus pilus*

*Centurion*

*Optio*

*Legionary soldiers*

*Praefectus castrorum*

*Tribune*

*Legatus*

*Primus pilus*

# ROMAN DEFENCES

*Roman fort*

**R**oman forts all over the Empire used a similar design. They were first laid out with earth ramparts, timber gates and timber walls. Once the army decided to make its position permanent, stone walls, gateways and towers were built, replacing the temporary ones. A typical fort was laid out in a grid pattern, like many Roman towns. Buildings were linked by wide roads, leading from the headquarters in the middle of the fort to the commander's house and the four main gates. Barracks, granaries, storehouses, workshops and a bathhouse were all contained within the fort's walls.

Headquarters

Gateway

Barracks

LINES OF DEFENCE
Fort walls were surrounded by ditches filled with spikes and ankle-breaking timbers. Deep holes were dug too, containing sharp stakes called 'lilies'. These formed the first line of defence for forts in the most threatened areas and the only way in was through the four guarded gateways.

Wooden spikes like this modern reconstruction (below) provided good defence against attacking soldiers and cavalry.

## HEADQUARTERS

The headquarters (right) were the administrative and ceremonial centre of the fort. A paved courtyard was surrounded by offices and a verandah. This led to an inner room where the legion's standards and a shrine were kept. Beneath this was a strongroom where soldiers' savings, valuables and the legion's weapons and armour were stored. The largest room in the headquarters was a hall, where parades took place on special occasions and where the commander could address his troops.

## TRAJAN'S COLUMN

This 30 m-high column in Rome was created in AD 113 to honour Emperor Trajan's victories in central Europe. It is covered in carvings of soldiers fighting and building forts. In this detail (below) troops are pictured digging foundations and building the walls of a fort.

*Room containing standards and shrine*

*Courtyard and verandah*

# TRAINING

*New recruits in training*

Even when not on campaign, the Roman army continually practised drills and tactics. Many Roman forts had a large open space within their walls, close to the headquarters building. This was used as a parade ground where parades and kit-inspections regularly took place. Parades on important occasions were particularly elaborate and were opportunities for new recruits to learn discipline and recognise battle commands. New recruits also took part in daily weapons practice, using wooden swords and wicker shields (right). Long marches carrying heavy loads and building camps and forts helped keep soldiers fit for battle.

*Reconstruction of a Roman practice shield*

## SHIELDS
The Romans used their shields to crash into opponents. They then stabbed them repeatedly with their sword or gladius. This meant that shield practice was an important part of training.

*Wicker*

*Hide*

*Marching camp*

## MARCHING CAMPS
On well-made Roman roads, heavily-laden soldiers could march about 40 km in a day. They sheltered overnight in temporary 'marching camps'. These were always laid out in the same way as a fort, with the commander's tent in the centre. A camp for an entire legion needed 800 tents. Half the legion stood on guard while the others dug a ditch and earth rampart all around the camp.

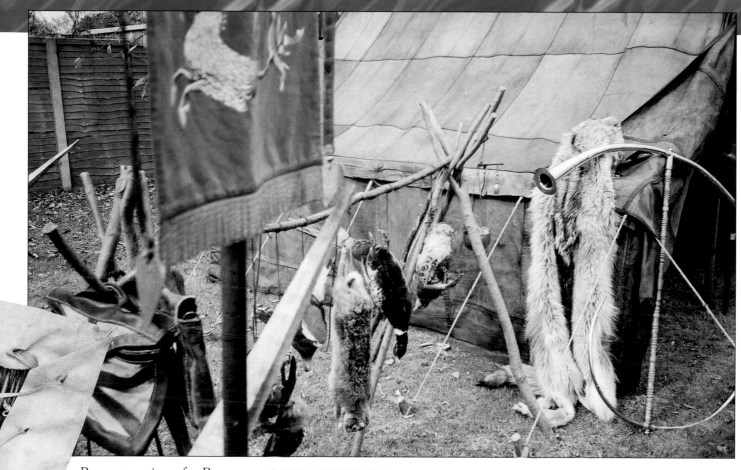

*Reconstruction of a Roman tent and the result of a successful hunt*

## TENTS AND FOOD

When on the march, each soldier carried enough food for three days. They ate mostly bread, cheese, lentils and beans, but this could be supplemented by rabbits and other hunted animals (above). Army tents were made of leather stretched over wooden poles. Eight men shared each tent.

## BATTLE FORMATIONS

Practising battle tactics and shield formations were an important element of the Roman army's success. When attacking fortifications, troops would move into the tortoise position, or *testudo* (right), and could protect themselves from the arrows and missiles raining down on them by interlocking their shields above their heads. A wedge-shaped formation called the 'pig's head', or *caput porcinum*, was used to thrust into enemy lines and crush them with a wall of shields.

*Centurion*

*Reconstruction of a testudo*

# LIFE IN THE LEGION

Coin bearing a
legion's standard

Life as a Roman soldier was tough. The risk of injury or death in battle or through disease was considerable. Army discipline was harsh – soldiers could be flogged for theft and crucified for more serious crimes. Men could not even marry while in the army. So why did they enlist? The pay was regular and fair and many soldiers managed to save part of their earnings. This meant that they were better off than many normal Roman citizens. For a legionary, the army was a lifelong career. They signed up for 25 years service and, inevitably, many died before they were able to retire. Those that survived were given land and money upon retirement.

Reconstruction of a
legionary's uniform

Legionary with full equipment

Helmet with
neck protector

Body armour
(lorica segmentata)

Bronze
cooking pan

Kit bag

Javelin
(pila)

Digging tool
(dolabra)

Dagger

Sword (gladius)

Sandals
(caligae)

Wool tunic under
the armour

Shield (scutum)

Mess rooms

Storeroom

Hearth

Bunk

## BARRACKS AND MESS ROOMS

Each barrack block in a fort contained ten pairs of rooms called messes (left). Eight men shared each pair of rooms. In one were bunks where the soldiers slept and there may have been a small hearth for warmth. The other room was used to store clothing, armour, equipment and personal possessions. There was also an area for preparing food.

*Roman centurion helmet with eagle decoration*

*Denarius coin depicting the Roman Emperor Nero*

## PAY DAY

Legionaries were paid around 225 denarii (silver pieces) and auxiliaries were paid 150 denarii per year in the 1st century AD. Pay could be deducted if a unit had appeared cowardly in battle and soldiers could be put on half pay for a year as punishment for serious offences.

## HELMETS

Roman helmets (left) were a sign of a solder's rank and were vital protection against enemy blows in battle.

## TIME OFF

There was probably not a lot of free time for Roman soldiers. They could relax playing dice, cleaning armour, mending equipment and taking turns to cook. Swords and daggers were sharpened and helmets polished. Gaming boards have been found in several Roman forts with counters made of stone, glass, or pottery.

# INTO BATTLE

*Typical Roman battle formation*

Ancient Rome was wealthy and could afford to keep a large permanent army as well as building the roads and ships necessary to send forces all over the Empire, wherever and whenever they were needed.

There were about 150,000 legionaries in the army and they proved to be a well-drilled and disciplined force in battle. They formed tight ranks and acted as a single force, legionaries to the front and centre, reserve troops behind them. The auxiliary soldiers (see page 40) flanked either side. Moving towards the enemy, legionaries threw their javelins at a range of 25 m. Then, protected by their shields, they advanced, engaging the enemy at close quarters with swords and daggers. Most of the forces encountered by the Romans were not so well trained or disciplined and this assured Rome of success in extending its Empire.

*Legatus and other senior officers*
*Legionaries*
*Cavalry*
*Auxiliaries*
*Enemy*

### BATTLE TACTICS
Roman commanders had an almost scientific approach to war. They did not believe in wasting their men in headlong charges at the enemy; instead, they considered the layout of the battlefield, direction of the wind and even the time of day. Julius Caesar, one of Rome's most successful generals, advised his soldiers to attack when the sun was behind them, so that its rays would dazzle and confuse the enemy.

Onagers were used against enemy fortifications. On one end of the large arm was a sling containing rocks.

A counterweight was dropped at the other end of the onager, pivoting the arm and launching the rocks.

Two men were needed to operate a ballista (below): one to winch and the other to load and fire the large crossbow.

### SIEGES

The Roman army was expert at siege warfare, using onagers, seige towers, catapults and ballistas to pound enemy fortifications and city walls.

*Onager*

*Ballista*

*Aquilifer*

*Imago standard bearer*

*Signifer*

*Cornicen*

### STANDARD BEARERS

As the legionaries went into battle, there were soldiers amongst them whose job it was to be seen rather than to fight. These were the standard bearers (right). They often wore animal skins over their heads to make them look more ferocious and imposing. It was seen as the greatest disgrace to lose your standard to the enemy in battle, so these men were well protected by soldiers willing to lay down their lives for the standard.

An aquilifer was the most important standard bearer as his standard showed the imperial eagle, or *aquila*.

A signifer wore a bearskin and a shirt of brass scales. He was the standard bearer for a century of legionaries.

The imago was a standard showing the emperor's head on it, a symbol of his presence and to keep up morale.

A cornicen was a horn player who gave signals during battle.

# AUXILIARIES

Roman warships were armed with a bronze prow to smash into enemy boats.

Prow

Auxiliary soldier

Bronze helmet

Chain mail over a tunic

Auxiliary soldiers were originally recruited into the Roman army from non-Roman nations. Auxiliary means 'helper' and these soldiers assisted legionaries by providing specialised fighting techniques and extra manpower. *Cohors equitata* were mixed regiments of infantry and cavalrymen. Auxiliary soldiers were usually posted abroad in case they were more loyal to their own nation than to Rome. After an auxiliary was discharged from the army he was presented with a bronze certificate, like a medal, and granted Roman citizenship.

Decorated oval shield

Thrusting spear (hasta)

A wooden tower at each end of the deck provided platforms for soldiers to shelter from enemy arrows.

Wooden tower

Auxiliary cavalryman

Four-cornered saddle

### ROMAN WARSHIPS

In 54 BC, Julius Caesar had 600 special landing craft and 28 warships built for the invasion of Britain. These vessels were wider and lower so they could be loaded quickly and carry troops right onto the beaches.

### AUXILIARY WEAPONS AND TECHNIQUES

Many of the auxiliary weapons and fighting techniques were adapted from their native lands: horseback warriors came from conquered tribes in Gaul (France); most auxiliary archers originated in the Middle East and slingshot experts armed with lethal stone 'bullets' came from the southern Mediterranean.

### AUXILIARY CAVALRY

Auxiliary cavalry were known as *alae*, or wings, because they were fast-moving and fought on either side of the foot soldiers. They were also used as scouts and escorts for convoys. Roman saddles had four horn-shaped corners to hold the rider in place.

# TIMESPAN

**3100 BC**
Upper and lower Egypt are unified by Menes, founder of the first Egyptian dynasty in Memphis.

**2700 BC**
The Sumerian/Egyptian culture starts to grow. The Sumerians use four-wheeled carts drawn by asses in warfare for the first time around 2500 BC.

*Sumerian cart*

**2682-2181 BC**
Old Kingdom period of Egypt.

**2400 BC**
Rise of Canaanite power based in Ebla (Syria).

**2040-1786 BC**
Middle Kingdom period of Egypt. The nation is reunited and now centred in Thebes.

**2100 BC**
The Sumerian civilisation is at its height.

**1576 BC**
The Hyksos are driven out of Egypt. Nubia (northern Sudan) is conquered by the Egyptians.

**1567-1085 BC**
New Kingdom period of Egypt.

**1475 BC**
The Hittites and Egyptians come into conflict over Palestine and Syria.

**1375 BC**
The Hittites expand and overrun the Babylonian Empire up to Syria.

**1320-1200 BC**
Pharaoh Seti I and Pharaoh Rameses II repel the Hittite threat and maintain Egyptian power.

*Statue of Rameses II*

**1273 BC**
The Hittites and Assyrians go to war resulting in the decline of the Hittite Empire.

**1200 BC**
The Sea Peoples invade Cyprus, Palestine and Syria. They are halted on the borders of Egypt around 1190 BC, by Rameses III. The Hittite Empire falls apart under the invasion of the Sea Peoples.

**1100 BC**
The pharaohs' powers are in decline and the Egyptian military splits the Empire into small states.

**900-750 BC**
Rise of the Greek city-states.

*Ancient Greek shield, sword and helmet*

**509 BC**
Founding of the republic of Rome.

**546-449 BC**
The Persian Wars. The Persians try to invade Greece but are driven back at the battle of Salamis in 480 BC.

**477-405 BC**
The golden age of Athens as a Greek city-state.

**446-404 BC**
The Peloponnesian War between Athens and Sparta. The turning point was the siege of Syracuse in 415 BC when the Spartans helped the Syracuse garrison to defeat the Athenian navy.

**382-336 BC**
Weakness of the Greek city-states allowed Philip II of Macedonia the opportunity to make himself master of Greece.

**334-332 BC**
The conquests of Alexander the Great. His last great battle, at Hydaspes in 326 BC, is against the Indian King Porus. The King uses elephants in his forces and Alexander is so impressed by them he eventually incorporates them into his own army.

*Statue of Alexander the Great*

**146 BC**
The Romans destroy Corinth and make Greece and Macedonia into one province.

**73-71 BC**
Spartacus, an ex-gladiator, leads a slave revolt over their harsh treatment. After several months, the rebellion is crushed by Roman General Pompey. The captured rebels are crucified along the length of the Appian way, a road leading to Rome.

**59-51 BC**
Julius Caesar wars with the Gauls in France. The Gauls adapt well to being conquered and many take on Roman ways and learn Latin. Eventually the Gauls are allowed to govern themselves and become trusted allies of Rome.

**55 BC**
Julius Caesar leads an unsuccessful invasion of Britain.

**49 BC**
Julius Caesar marches into Rome to take control of the Empire and goes on to defeat Pompey's armies in Greece, Egypt, Asia and Spain.

**44 BC**
Julius Caesar is murdered outside the Senate House in Rome.

**44-31 BC**
Civil war in the Roman Empire between Consul Octavian and one of the Roman leaders, Mark Anthony. Anthony is defeated by Octavian and his admiral Agrippa in the harbour at Actium (in present day Greece).

**27 BC**
Octavian is renamed Augustus and becomes the first Roman Emperor.

*Emperor Augustus*

**AD 4**
Probable date of the birth of Jesus Christ.

**AD 9**
Germanic tribes destroy three Roman legions in the forest of Teutoburger, stopping Rome's advance across the Rhine.

**AD 43**
Under the orders of Emperor Claudius, the Roman army invades Britain.

**AD 61**
Boudicca, a tribal queen, leads a rebellion in eastern Britain but it is defeated by the Romans.

**AD 101-107**
Emperor Trajan goes to war in Dacia (Romania).

**AD 122**
Emperor Hadrian builds a huge fortified wall across the north of Britain.

**AD 286**
Emperor Diocletian reforms the Roman army and splits the Empire into east and west. Each is ruled by an emperor and his junior but in AD 305-337 these power sharing arrangements break down.

**AD 312**
Emperor Constantine becomes the Roman Empire's single ruler. The Empire becomes Christian after Constantine's conversion in AD 313.

**AD 407**
Last Roman troops withdraw from Britain.

**AD 410**
The fall of Rome after it is sacked by Alaric, King of the Visigoths.

*Fall of Rome*

# GLOSSARY

**Argive** A type of shield carried by a Greek infantryman.

**Ballista** A giant crossbow.

**Baton** A short stick carried to use as a weapon.

**Battering ram** A heavy beam used to batter down gates and walls during a seige.

**Centurion** A Roman army officer in charge of a century.

**Century** A unit in a Roman army consisting of eighty men.

**Chain mail** Flexible armour made of joined metal links or scales.

**Chariot** A horse-drawn vehicle used in battle.

**City-states** Independent cities and the surrounding areas over which their governments rule.

**Civilisation** A society governed by cultural and political ideals.

**Cohort** One of ten divisions which made up a Roman legion.

**Conscript** Someone who is forced to fight in an army.

**Consul** One of the two highest officials elected each year to rule over the republic of Rome.

**Conturbenium** The smallest unit in the Roman army, consisting of eight men.

**Empire** A collection of peoples and territories under the rule of a single person or state.

**Greave** A piece of armour that protects the shin from the knee to the ankle.

**Hoplite** A member of the Greek infantry.

**Humty** The name given to the long-haired Hittite warriors. It means 'women soldiers'.

**Infantry** Soldiers who fight on foot with carried weapons.

**Khopesh** An Egyptian curved sword.

**Legion** The largest unit in the Roman army, consisting of around 4,800 men.

**Mercenaries** Men hired and paid to fight for a foreign army.

**Nomadic** A people or tribe who move from place to place to find food.

**Peloponnesian War** A war from 431-404 BC in which the ancient Greek city-state of Athens was defeated by a group of rival states.

**Phalanx** A battle formation used by the ancient Greeks and Macedonians. It consisted of hoplites pointing spears out from a wall of overlapping shields.

**Prow** The front part of a ship's hull.

**Onager (1)** A wild ass found in Central Asia.

**Onager (2)** A large siege engine used to hurl rocks.

**Pharaoh** The title of ancient Egyptian kings.

**Poleis** The Greek word for 'city-states'.

**Punic Wars** The three wars (264-241 BC, 218-201 BC and 149-146 BC) in which ancient Rome defeated and eventually destroyed Carthage.

**Quiver** A case for arrows.

**Rampart** A fortification consisting of a steep bank, often topped with a fence or wall.

**Regiment** A group of soldiers under one commander.

**Republic** A state in which the people or their elected representatives hold power.

**Scribe** A person employed to write down what is spoken by his or her employer.

**Siege** The surrounding and blockading of a fortification or town in order to capture it.

**Slinger** Someone who uses a sling to hurl projectiles.

**Tunic** A loose-fitting garment extending to the knees.

**Tribute** A payment from one state to another.

**Vizier** A high officer in Muslim government.

# INDEX

Page numbers in bold refer to illustrations

# BOOK HOUSE

Look out for these other exciting titles from Book House

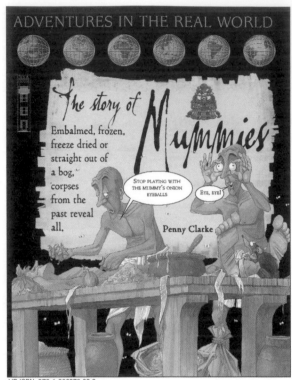

HB ISBN: 978-1-906370-02-2
PB ISBN: 978-1-906370-03-9

## ADVENTURES IN THE REAL WORLD

Travel through time into a world of discovery, disaster and adventure. Stunningly illustrated throughout, with maps and cutaway drawings, these titles provide an invaluable insight into events that helped shape the world we know.

- Hardback £12.99
- Paperback £6.99
- 282 x 219 mm; 64pp
- Interest 8+; Reading age 9+
- KS 2/3
- Superb full-colour illustrations
- Informative text
- Contents, glossary and index

Penny Clarke

HB ISBN: 978-1-905638-16-1
PB ISBN: 978-1-905638-17-8

Penny Clarke

HB ISBN: 978-1-905638-02-4
PB ISBN: 978-1-905638-03-1

Penny Clarke

HB ISBN: 978-1-906370-00-8
PB ISBN: 978-1-906370-01-5

Doomed Ships

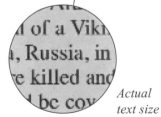

*Actual text size*

Available from all good bookshops
www.book-house.co.uk
or, for a catalogue, write to Book House, 25 Marlborough Place, Brighton, BN1 1UB